Modern Psalms
IN SEARCH OF PEACE AND JUSTICE

Dwight L. Wilson

ILLUSTRATIONS
Nancy Marstaller

FRIENDS UNITED PRESS

Copyright © 2017 by Friends United Press

All rights reserved. No part of this work may be reproduced or transmitted in any form or by any means, electronic or mechanical, including photocopying and recording, or by any information storage or retrieval system, except as may be expressly permitted by the 1976 Copyright act or in writing from the publisher. Requests for permission should be addressed in writing to Friends United Press.

Friends United Press
101 Quaker Hill Drive
Richmond, IN 47374

Wilson, Dwight L., 1948-
Modern Psalms in Search of Peace and Justice/ by Dwight L. Wilson.

ISBN-10: 0-944350-31-3
ISBN-13: 978-0-944350-31-7

Introduction

At least since kindergarten, I have recognized a living relationship with the Holy One. It was during our first year of formal schooling that we were taught to sing, "Jesus loves me, this I know, for the Bible tells me so." After school I said to myself, "That's silly; I don't need the Bible to know that."

In my early twenties, I was told a living personal relationship with God is the essence of mysticism, but few labels intrigue me.

My wife, Diane, also lives a centered life. In the autumn of 2015, Diane suggested we try our hands at writing psalms. Early in this spiritual discipline, I decided to write a sufficient number of psalms to warrant publishing a celebratory book for my fiftieth anniversary as a minister. I am a person who uses my own history, as well as that of my ancestors, in writing historical fiction, public speaking, and even dinner table conversation. No time period was left off the table. Also, I have read the Old and New Testaments cover to cover nine times. Independently, I have read most sections scores of times. Yet these psalms are not intended to be facsimiles of the originals and are influenced by studies of other spiritual approaches. My psalms are personal expressions of my relationship with the Supreme Being, written, without artifice, to the Holy One. Believing that Truth is non-sectarian, I cross artificial lines.

I was my parents' first child. I was also the first grandchild and nephew on the side that dominated my formative years. In many ways I was "the golden child." There were no perks. My family celebrated responsibility. That I was also academically gifted, and came early to leadership positions, increased my position's weight: I was charged with being an example for the relatives whose births followed mine. It was natural for me to fall in love with the old song, "A Charge to Keep I Have."

By my senior year in high school, I had held several prominent leadership positions, including Chairman of Explorer Scout Region IV—Ohio, Kentucky, and West Virginia. I had also been invited to the White House by Lady Bird Johnson, and selected as one of America's Top 11 Teenagers by a committee of national magazine editors.

April 15, 1966, changed everything. With the secret goal of finding a new girlfriend, I traveled from my birthplace in Middletown, Ohio, to attend a Baptist convention in Toledo. It was there that I received and accepted a call to the ministry.

When I returned home, my announcement was not well-received. Perhaps my mother's mom summarized it best, "Any fool can be a preacher." Not only was she contrasting my calling to my previous declaration that I was going to be the first attorney in family history, but she also agreed with bluesman Son House's words, "I'm goin' be a Baptist preacher . . . just so I won't have to work."

The family understanding of the ministry fell far short of mine, which itself has continued to develop. Interestingly, the reception was positive when I joined Quakerism, the ancestral faith of my paternal grandmother's people. William Penn was first cousins with Rachel Penn Bradshaw, one of my ninth-great-grandmothers.

I have served in traditional ministry roles as pastor, theology instructor, assistant chaplain at a liberal arts college, and General Secretary of my denomination (Friends General Conference). My ministry has also been extended as humanities teacher, dean, head of school, non-profit executive, and board trustee. In my understanding, the ministry, like wearing one's skin, is an assignment that has no time off.

Greatly coloring my psalms are several struggles in which I've participated. The first was trying to find a way out of the projects of Middletown, Ohio, when neither of my parents had advanced past tenth grade. The challenges continued as I worked full-time in each of the seven years that I attended college and graduate school. Almost as soon as I graduated with my Masters Degree in Divinity, I had to help my mother die when she was barely forty-four years old. Over time, I have presided over a number of funerals for those close to me—my father's as well as my mother's, three grandparents, fifteen aunts and uncles, three cousins who died young, and several friends. I've known the pain of divorce, and losing a never-to-be-forgotten baby.

I have also been a volunteer since my teenage years, walking with others in their struggles. Even while working as an executive, I averaged no less than eight hours a week with such organizations as Haverford College, Rancocas Friends School, Hospice, the Boys Club, Afri-Male Institute, American Friends Service Committee, Medford Leas Continuing Care Community, Big Brothers and Big Sisters, and the YMCA.

After retirement, I stepped up my volunteering hours, working as an Ann Arbor Human Rights Commissioner, as Clerk of the Earlham School of Religion Board of Advisors, as a trustee with Safe House Center (anti-domestic abuse and sexual assault), a tutor with SOS (homeless children), a trustee with Student Advocacy Center (reducing school suspensions and expulsions), a deliverer with Meals on Wheels, and my special weekly project—over six years of Monday mornings holding babies in the C.S. Mott Children's Hospital pediatric cardiac ward. This last is a place where we annually lose about thirty babies to chronic heart disease. Nurses, doctors, and parents have referred to me as a "baby-whisperer." I do know how to whisper to them, but do not pretend I can calm all babies.

I am a practicing mystic who has experienced joys and pains, yet always been carried by the Holy One.

Dwight L. Wilson
2/15/17

Modern Psalms
IN SEARCH OF PEACE AND JUSTICE

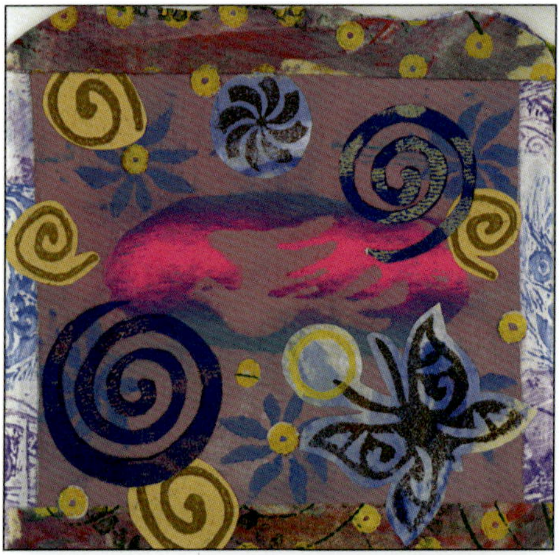

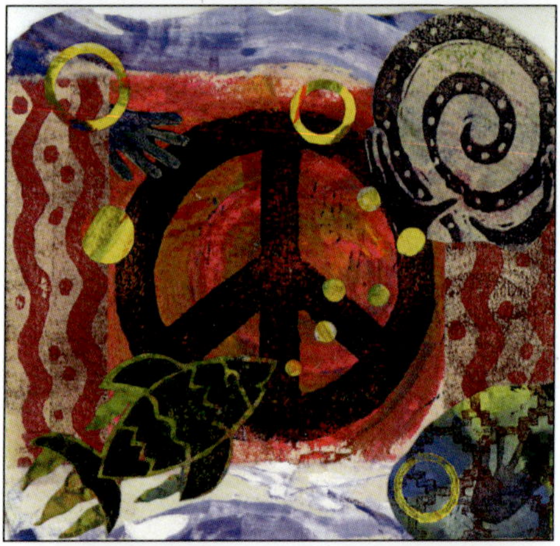

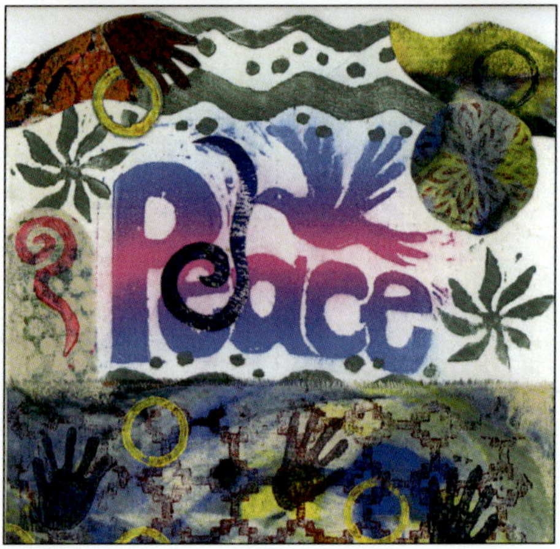
Peace

Psalm 1

THEY CALL YOU by many names:
Allah, God, Great Spirit, Jah, Jehovah,
Moneto, Nyame, Shango, Tenaya,
The Lord, Yahweh, and thousands more.
Caring for all, You answer to none.
"I am who I am," and
"I shall be who I shall be,"
speak to the essence of Your matchless power.
Many of us claim You are on our side,
ignoring the fact that You are a side.
Far too often we fight against Your desire,
killing our siblings while mouthing
the pursuit of peace.
Forgive us the debts that we accumulate
and nonbelievers assign to Your account.
For our own benefit we have betrayed
Your good name,
casting shame on all under the sun.

Psalm 2

ON MY JOURNEY to You, I was distracted
by the sea and mountains.
Foolishly, I dismissed
clouds traveling
in indescribable shapes.
I tried to describe those
that seemed to invite my efforts.
In defiance, they altered
their faces and went about their business.
For too long, my spiritual level
dwelt in what seemed fixed.
I missed that even rocks
are constantly in flux.
In ignorance I dared to claim that

You do not change.

What is prayer other than effort
to get You to change
what appears to be Your plan?
"If it is possible, remove this cup..."
Help me escape crutches
in whatever form they appear.
Help me respect the beauty
in the clouds as they cross the skies,
while making alliances only
with those who share
their present understanding.

Psalm 3

BENEATH the half moon,
we realize that Your desire
is for our whole heart.
When complete is possible
never are You satisfied
with tiny bits of effort.
We remove our eyes
from that which is lurking
in the shadows of the Center.
Blessed is obedience
to the One who is our all.
Through serving You we understand
that all of creation is worthy of respect,
the future as well as the past and present,
our neighbors as well as our families,
our enemies as well as our friends.

Psalm 4

WE DUG in our heels,
two steps from the brink
of yet another chasm.
The fear of a concentrated push
made us tremble—but not surrender.
Denials of access did not hurt us most.
Our pain was born of the lie
that the playing field was level.
Trying another way, we discovered
walls that were constructed
high and venomously.
Still we prepared to scale the bulwark.
You arrived riding an ocean of love.
Proudly we sing Your praises.
We have been chosen as the ones
to help build a pathway to the stars.

Psalm 5

FROM OUR MOST BELOVED
to the hills themselves,
we see aging.
You are the exception.
Your spirit is timeless yet right on time,
a living contradiction.
Tenderly You call us
to live contrary to the world.
You expect us
to walk away from violence,
be willing to give all that others might live,
forgive even the greatest betrayals.
To set aside reason
in favor of obedience
takes more than will.
It takes surrender of self
for the greater good.
Help us rise to acceptance
even as we suffer ridicule.
Let us feel the pressure of our peers
less than breath influences the ocean.

Psalm 6

AFTER MY LEAVES had seemed to wither,
You have caused fruit to blossom.
I do not try to explain
what appears a miracle.
My goal is complete gratitude.
Your ways are
beyond my comprehension,
Your grace, so magnificent.
I sing Your song,
assured that You can hear
even unspoken lyrics.

Forgive me for allowing the Truth
to pass by me time and again.
I was afraid to acknowledge
what any fool could see.
Now I testify for all to hear:
the One who judges all
and has no need of references,
has acquitted me
of what I thought was a death sentence.
The road ahead has been cleared
for my continued journey.

Psalm 7

YOUR SONG knows nothing
of the human calendar.
Each day is a holy day
inviting us to honor You
with our commitment.
Our allegiance is to the One
who has made us
and continues to sustain us.
Help us work past the set-asides
that encourage occasional
or sporadic good behavior.
There is no beauty in the freedom
to sit down on the job.
If we practice lukewarm effort,
too many of Your children
will live and die
in need of our assistance.
May we hold up Your banner in all we do,
wear it as lightly as freckles—not as burdensome
as carrying the world's weight.

Psalm 8

WE CELEBRATE Your will
by remembering those who died young.
We pause in silence
recalling the ones who died:
as soldiers in avoidable wars;
as gangsters senselessly killing each other;
of chronic illnesses whose cure
was within focused reach;
by ever-devolving weapons
in shopping malls, theaters,
schools, churches, and parking lots;
as young idealists killed
while marching for peace and justice.
Oh Lord, we acknowledge
our failures and ask three questions.
What have we done to protect young life?
What are we doing to protect young life?
How have we failed You?
May we find the courage to rise up and
leave our position as accomplices.

Psalm 9

I SEE MY SIBLINGS sick and shut in,
surfing inches from sorrow.
Yours is a comforting presence,
a mighty strength in times of need.
Although I am not nearly
as lonely as a lunar eclipse,
and my health remains,
I, too, welcome Your love.
Sweep me into Your constant joy.
Help me remember
that we are never
self-sustaining islands.
Each of us climbs ladders
steadied by Your grace.
May I always strive to be a messenger
whose tidings bring peace.

Psalm 10

BLESSED IS THE ONE who remembers—
that all things are not acceptable.
The measure of Your children
is how well we can bridge the gap
between good intention and right practice.
I quiet myself and wait,
not for Your return
but for my own,
to Original Goodness.
Help me step away
from the righteous anger
that sometimes clouds my spirit.
Help me accept the joy Your love offers.

Psalm 11

PRAYING TO YOU

is neither words nor Quaker silence.
Prayer is listening
in the woods, or on a seat of pews,
on city streets, or in classrooms,
inside office buildings, or in cars.
I come to You who never leaves.
Holy One, speak
to me in ways of healing.
Help me reach out
to those who have misused me,
even as I embrace
those who have comforted me.
Your world is a circle
always leading to divinity.
May my prayer and Your will
be one and the same.

Psalm 12

THE WORD CAME that I am newly
a motherless child.
A loving mother, or even grandmother,
is a special grace.
Her death can crush.
Thank You for taking her place
in holding me.
As I had been taught, I turned to You.
The faded world took on new light.
I am made able to celebrate her life
and appreciate Yours.
So long as memory and love lasts
it is not over.

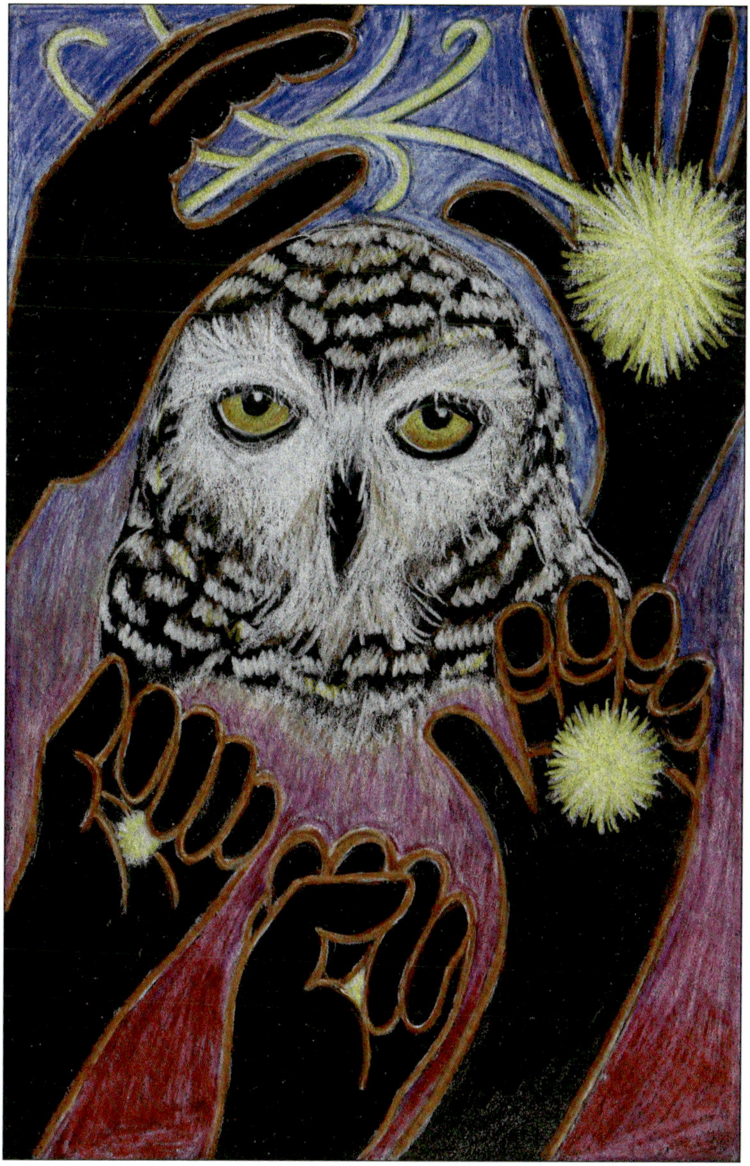

Psalm 13

FOR MOST, it would be easiest
to see You perform
solo on the universal stage
while we sit in the audience, eating popcorn.
That is not the design.
We are in this love together:
You as Spirit Prodding,
we as physical beings charged
with improving unfinished work.
We seek to perfect Your creation.
With wars and terrorist attacks
all across the globe,
and hatred running rampant,
apathy is not a choice.

We must act, or close the road
to our descendants' survival.
Through Your call to love
You bring an arsenal of compassion.
Help us sing in tune,
spiritually rising to conquer evil,
fortifying the world
with our unwavering love.

Psalm 14

THEY ARE CARELESS with our lives,
killing those who fit a certain stereotype
and daring to name immorality, patriotism.
They attempt to mask
gross misconduct as being
in line with their religion.
We matter both on the streets
and inside skyscrapers,
in hoodies and pin-striped suits.
Is there no end to cold-blooded murder?
You, the Lord of all, have sent
representatives, elected and otherwise.

Their quick-time marching orders
demand they speak clearly
about their responsibility,
and use their courts
with community safety
as an irrefutable need.
Will no one come to our rescue?
Help them stop their posturing
and blaming the victims.
Teach them to be human enough
to realize that public cowardice
is unacceptable in Your eyes.

Psalm 15

YOUR SWEET SONG
touches my ears and soul.
Thank You that my life is not like cheap ink
running down a rain soaked page,
losing both sheen and meaning
because it was not built to last.
I follow Your direction
through verdant valleys
and soot-stained concrete canyons.
Dry my perspiration
with Your perfection.
If tears are my only moisture,
let their number fall short of inundation.
Teach me to walk on my own water,
straight into Your arms,
the only ones capable of embracing
all of creation at once.

21

Psalm 16

I HAVE WAITED to hear You
calling my name.
You have arrived in the quiet,
even as last night, inside the jostling crowd,
You whispered low.
Never alone, You and I,
serving the same children,
each created by Your passion,
each looking past
divisive and hate-filled lines drawn by race
and ethnicity, social class,
and other imagined distances.

In awe of You, I sing, bowing my head,
humbly acknowledging Your sovereignty
and my responsibility
to honor a world in need of repair.
From the edge of my own wounds,
I stride forward, confident
that You can heal all things.
When I listen to You,
my personal inability to master words
will be no impediment.
Your "yes" is my "I can."

Psalm 17

FORGIVE US our fragility.
We have received
our inheritance
in the softest age
since time's dawn.
Many have become so secure
in insecurity
that they can commit to nothing.
We see politicians flip flop
from long-held positions;
thriving businesses who received
burdensome concessions
abandon thousands of employees;
beloved players and coaches smile,
while leaving teams
that form the center
of our new religions;
parents discard their children.

Consistency is found only in Your love.
People do not need camels to be nomads
or refugee camps to be on the run.
We shamelessly flee
from lasting commitment.
Help us envision deeper lives.
Give us the courage and strength
to stand for something
beyond the moment.
Let us embrace
Your unchanging love:
the only certainty in our lives.

Psalm 18

WE COME TOGETHER
in families of all varieties known to love.
Some of us live far from the standard issue.
It is You who have made us,
not we ourselves.
"Just as I am,"
"Don't Make Me Over,"
old song titles that express our wishes
as well as our natures.
Though we have yet to move
over the rainbow, thank You
for not allowing the multi-colored arch
to fall upon us, or the melting pot
to consume us.
In this journey we lift our voices
to praise our shifting normals
and say, "Hallelujah!
The King is not dead!
Long live our families."

Psalm 19

WE MOVE in beauty
when we move with You.
Whether traveling
on superhighways,
over potholed pavements,
or forging new paths.
Through what we deem to be
no more than wilderness,
we stride naturally.
Despite temporarily
possessing a model's
well constructed beauty
or permanently
bearing deformities
that repel the shallow,
the faithful are gorgeous
to the indomitable core.

There is one true destination.
It is wallpapered with love,
not the greenbacks in which
our nation places trust.
There is one personal attraction,
the glow of compassion.
Give us the strength and wisdom
to avoid temptations
to pleasure ourselves,
comply with goose steps
of the rulers of darkness,
or shuffle in silence
that humors waiting wolves.
Help us stay in tune
with Your divine will.
Beauty is as beauty
radiates in Your name.

Psalm 20

IN YOUR HONOR we try
to live with the sustained power
of the best who have walked before us.
Our spiritual ancestors sometimes fell short,
but we believe they always
reached for the heights.
The way through the darkness
should not be tackled by seeing
the trees as individuals.
The wise see the forest as a whole.
I am not now, nor have I ever been, alone.
During human and spiritual bondage,
economic exploitation,
and all manner of evil,
You have been the Door to Justice.
Blessed is the song that
You have implanted in each heart.
We sing the right notes
whenever we obey the Righteous One.

Psalm 21

LOOKING BACK is the touchstone.
Looking forward is the vision.
You are in each moment,
whether it is bliss or pain.
Perhaps we err in dividing time
into units beyond day, night, and seasons.
Surely day in and day out,
the weight of our ancestors affects
the fate of our descendants.
Help us carry on as though we believe
in Your people, one folk indivisible,
bound by neither borders
made of sea, mountains,
nor falsely-drawn lines.
Help us be there when You need us most,
something we cannot presume to measure.
All we know is the call to worship is always,
and we will dwell in Your love forever.

Psalm 22

IN HONOR OF YOU, I respect my neighbor
though her speech and values make her
an example of what some call "the other."
I listen to his views even though they differ
from my father's and my own.
We walk together across a line of razors.
Our soles are as barefoot
as they were at birth.
That mine are calloused and theirs as soft
as royal tissue does not matter.
Together with you,
we make up a single-Parent family
whose living wish is for us
to love one another
as we have been loved.

Psalm 23

ON THE DAY of the earthquake,
the doubter has a change of mind,
looking up and begging
for divine assistance.
We do not blame the fearfully contrite
for accepting new light.
It is clear the world is filled
with ambushing catastrophes.
Help us address the climate change caused
by our carelessness and perpetuated
by shortsighted leaders.
Help us understand
the buck starts with the people.
We call Your name knowing
each hour is one of need,
and no elected official
can rescue us from ourselves.

Psalm 24

MAY WE TRANSFORM
our mistakes into blessings,
by lessons learned and applied in real time.
May we appreciate the hidden stars
for their unseen perfection.
It is not the cloudy night
that casts down the searching soul.
It is disrespecting goodness
that in the moment
is invisible to the naked eye.
Help those of us who see ourselves
as the children of sorrow honor blessings,
both on the wind and in the present hour.

Psalm 25

EPIC is the story from Slavery
and Original Jim Crow
through Classic Jim Crow
to the New Jim Crow.
Will the next movement be Resolution?
You have been with us
from the kidnapping of bodies
to the kidnapping of opportunities.
We do not pretend that Yours has been
the loudest music.
We contend that Yours has been
the sweetest music.
Watching them play the God card
and the race card has been painful.

You have cried
during our oppression
because our persecutors were also Yours.
Help our tormentors
perform Your music,
or at least understand the score
behind the symphony's creation.
"And it was good." It can still be good.
"Love your neighbor,"
as you want your beloved to be loved.
The commandment is for "justice and mercy."
Your compositions are divine
to the ears of the faithful.
May our performance be acceptable
in Your judgment.

Psalm 26

ONCE I WAS LOST in uncharted desert.
Now, like the waves
that follow a canoe
in placid waters,
Your love ripples my soul.
The depth of Your touch
is a mighty infusion of pure power.
I look to the shores of my life,
happy to be inside
this empowering channel.
I hear You say, "Arise and care
for my people as a whole.
Do not mimic the deceitful,
but beware of mouthing
eternal condemnation.

Let Me separate the obedient
from the mistaken.
Many a prodigal returns in glory."
Reminded that I am one of the measured,
I accept my calling as a follower.
Each season I hear the echoes
of Your mighty words
swirling from the stream
through a medley of trees
planted by the waters.
Whether the forest is
leaf-heavy or bony-branched,
You, my Protector, are evergreen.

Psalm 27

HUNCHED against the wind,
I wait for a subsiding's promise.
This is not my first storm.
You were there
in each previous pummeling.
Faith declares You are here still.
There is a howling
that makes speaking useless.
Even in my silence,
You are present, anchoring.
Without Your love
I would be blown off an ant hill.
Your grace amazes.
Sometimes help arrives
in surprising form.

In my mind, I see knights
in shining armor
or the cavalry cresting the hill.
Then I am rescued by a baby,
or someone elderly whom I thought
could not possibly know the way
to this new frontier.
More than once a person
whom I had vilified
has broken the enemy's role,
as if to say,
"Here am I. I have been sent."
Help me accept allies
from my blind side.
Help me remember
each time I tripped, I fell up.

Psalm 28

TENDER is the night of rescue,
regardless of the source of agony.
You are Redeemer
in the hour of needs, recognized or unseen.
May we always hear Your voice
above the cacophony of oppression.
The captives cry out seeking deliverance,
be it in the refugee camps,
orphanages or migrant fields,
while seeking employment,
or restricted to mental institutions,
struggling in homeless shelters,
or restrained in hospital wards,
incarcerated in prisons,
or simply trying to make life
in abandoned communities.
The bottom dwellers' souls
have a lover in You.
May we also prove ourselves friends.

41

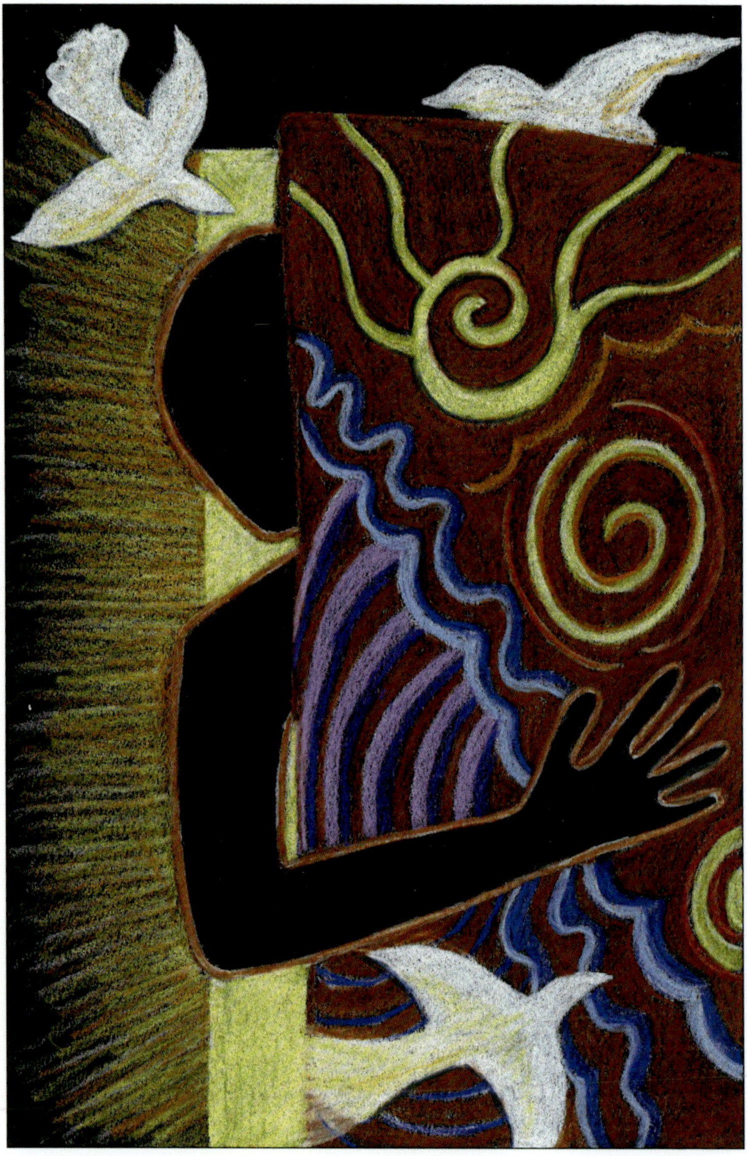

Psalm 29

THE HOLY ONE has offered an open door.
They insist on wandering
past freedom and living
in self-incarceration.
Anguish feeds
on the inability to forgive themselves
for actions they knew were wrong.
Shuffling feet and wringing hands
may calm the guilt-ridden
but cannot soothe victims.
Help us all sing a song of healing,
one whose substance is in doing
the right thing from here until eternity.

The story is told of Lot's wife,
who deserved to have her name passed down,
but finds it forgotten
by all of her descendants.

She was "turned into a pillar of salt."
Her crime was remembering
that even amidst evil,
memories of the faithful who stood firm
are praiseworthy.
Too often we have followed those
who choose to bury the past
and dishonor our ancestors.
No longer shall we cling to guilt
as though it were a life jacket.

Up and at it!
Though midnight, dawn awaits.
Your promise of redemption begins
with accepting responsibility.

Psalm 30

YOU BROUGHT US late to creation.
Like a wounded lover,
You told us to make it last.
We are the caretakers
for a million million years,
indebted not only to You
but to our ancestors,
the animals, rocks, sea, air,
and our undreamed progeny.
We cannot, in good faith,
take generations off
from focusing on our assignment.
We cannot justifiably hope
others can reverse our inattentiveness
and right a ship constructed
with wilful negligence.

To whom should we cry for mercy
when we have demonstrated so little?
Let us sing a new song
that is exemplary to the ears of all.
If we fight against You,
even if winning were possible,
we would lose.

Psalm 31

I CLOSE MY EYES to distractions,
confident Your guidance is coming.
Yesterday I was attacked
for unknown reasons
and struggled for understanding.
Today I am waiting
among other like-minded folk.
The opening way
in this Quaker meeting
brings together spirits
which rise to meet You,
each expecting a gathering of souls
at Your river of peace.

Solace drifts in currents,
rippling although the wind is still.
Our siblings are hard-pressed worldwide.
Without universal justice,
sustaining personal peace is impossible.
A raft of seekers moves imperceptibly,
yet deliberately forward.
Our destination is a place where energy
radiates before a luminous door.
Here is the seat of healing.
With love we purchase entry.
Behold the boundless neighborhood
of the Holy One!

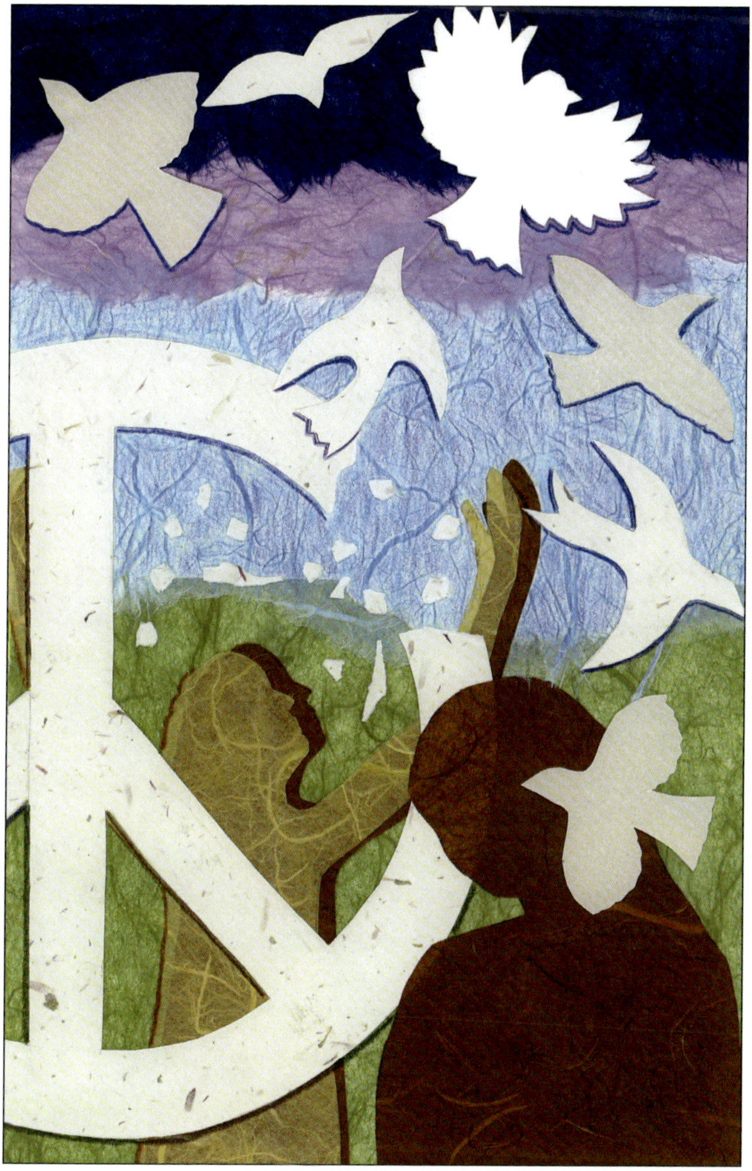

Psalm 32

I LOOKED toward the heavens
as though You were hiding
somewhere beyond the clouds.
I looked in the forests
as though only the wild things
understood your language.
I looked in churches
as though universally
they were sanctuaries.
I came to a corporate headquarters
where there were neither
offices nor cubicles.

To my surprise, it was in those
non-hallowed walls
You spoke Your truth.
"I have been with you
speaking through all your searches.
Always Present is my name."
Now I know that any separation
is mine alone, and beg Your forgiveness
for all the times
Your still, small voice went unheard
because my headstrong deafness
passed for Your unavailability.

Psalm 33

BREATHE INTO US the will and courage
to say, "I am who I am,"
whatever the cost.
Neither in hiding nor in coming forth
do we find a free item.
Instead of the cheapest cost available,
let us choose the best quality.
When we put ourselves behind ourselves
and walk in Your footsteps,
let us not worry
about filling Your shoes.
Our sole assignment is
to concentrate on
moving well in our own.

Psalm 34

FROM THE VIEW of the palm of Your hand,
it is possible to see eternity.
The consequence of obeying You
is as heartwarming
as a parent seeing a newborn
break into the light.
Your righteous voice resonates strength.
I am caught
by the One prepared
for any new world.

Psalm 35

THE BEST AFTERGLOW
is the awareness of First Glow.
Let's reject the question,
"What color is God?"
Making You in our image
is akin to thinking that
by writing fantasy
we can enable our own eternal life.
You are The Spirit
who originated colors,
the Shining Light
that illuminates the darkness,
the Darkness
that embraces all colors.

Let us approach You
after accepting the worthiness
of the whole spectrum.
Let us understand that original goodness
is found in our babies
and diligently work
to extend our nearness
to Your divine will
throughout our maturity.

Psalm 36

I REFUSE to live my life
like an inland gull
without inclination
to viewing the sea.
I will start from where I am
and set about searching
for what I believe You envision.
I will embrace more than safety,
taking risks to spread abundant life.
Though the ocean waves
may become threatened
by a series of storms,
I will fear nothing
but a self-stunted life.
May all my gifts and talents
be appreciated and polished.

Psalm 37

THE GAME OF PREDICTING

where the Holy Spirit
will lead us tomorrow
is a fool's practice.
One is the Master.
Perhaps disciples
following faithful scouts
through changing landscapes
best describes our journey.
Yes, there are trusted
markers pointing forward,
but the surprises
make all the difference.
We are the fearless,
listeners who hear
a Siren's safety song.

Psalm 38

MY ALLEGIANCE will not go
to the pentagonal gods:
money, sports, power,
popularity, and comfort.
I will accept no idols.
Life itself shall not prevent me
from Your appointed hour
of distilling love that flows
like a pure waterfall
in the rainy season.
I am the child called
to obey before conception,
the adult You asked to follow
before immaturity
had vanished in the mist.

May my mind be open
to remembering
that the way was designed
for true inclusion, and may
my actions focus on healing.
May I harmonize
only with Your songs.
When I stray off key,
forgive me and teach me
the way back to Wholeness.

Psalm 39

I LOOK TO JESUS
who proved himself
both Son and a friend.
He was my first hero.
Although many have betrayed
His name, His honor remains
unblemished by lies.
His servant, the Advocate,
continually reveals
the way to healing.
Divinely we have been carried
through uncounted decades
of deliberate dreariness

and blinding blizzards
where so-called leaders
exploited the people
while enriching their
bank accounts and reputations.
Forgive me when I
over-respect evil
as though it is too formidable
to challenge with hope.
The Lamb's song is victorious
even when death comes calling.
Help us voice our appreciation of grace
for the tiniest gift.

Psalm 40

ON MY ROAD to nowhere, I turned back.
In the moment of enlightenment
You were there.
As I matured, I realized
that during my lost period
You had been within,
calling in a still, small voice
unrecognizable by those
who choose not to hear.
Forgive me my overbearing pride
even as you forgive those
who learned self-hatred,
thus despising gifts that You had awarded.

Society teaches
that one from my background
is best seen as an outcast.

Thank You
for Your unedited praise messages
far beyond pages, screens,
factories, offices,
shelters, courtrooms, and prisons.
I hear them validating my essence,
clearing the way
for each wounded return.

Psalm 41

I OPEN MY EYES
from deepest prayer
and find snowflakes,
like stardust, swirling
on a full moon night.
The earth still holds fall's warmth.
These flakes will dissolve
like the dreams of children
in inferior schools
who are redirected
toward structured limits
that should shame adults.
The natural hurdles
we shall overcome.
The ones that we make
may trip generations.
We are aligned at the Center.

Help us to both accept
seasonal changes
and establish justice
in our children's lives.
Help us celebrate
the arts as much as
we kiss science and math,
lionize skills,
responsibility,
and resourcefulness,
as much as we cheer
reading and writing.
Your divine wholeness
heals broken circles.

Psalm 42

MY NEIGHBOR speaks of shame
for his ancestors' wrongs
but claims no shame
for the hand he was dealt.
Holding all aces
leaves little chance
for the ones waiting
for their first fair deal.
We do not ask our neighbor
to embrace her guilt.
Guilt is a tree of death.
We prefer abundant life
at a table shared by all.

You are the Deity of Justice.

Blessed be the outcasts,
for they shall be supported.

Blessed be the overlooked,
for they shall be watched over.

Blessed be nature,
for through showing respect
we shall be sustained.

Blessed be the privileged,
for they have been called
to comfort the outcasts.

Psalm 43

THE GREATEST BLINDNESS
does not belong to the sightless.
They are forced to measure by heart.
What burdens us in our search
for Your living will,
is the lack of vision of those
empowered to control,
and our fickle willingness
to trust the vanity
of self-proclaimed experts.
Truth known experientially
outshines intellectual theories.
Help us find our way to You.
We are not made less
by our disabilities.
We are made much more
by our willingness
to act as caregivers
for each of our siblings.

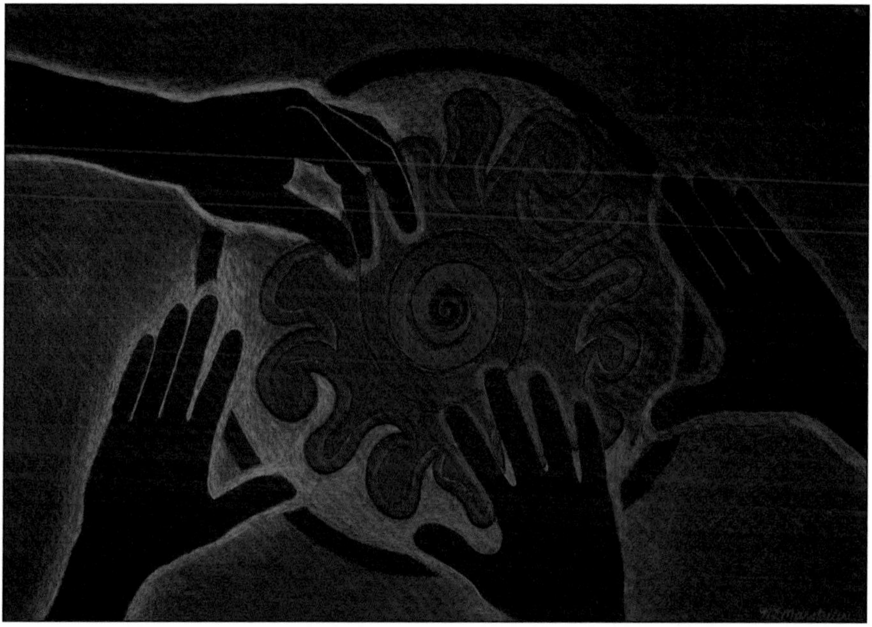

Psalm 44

I STOOD in a flood,
water fallen from my own eyes.
Mire lured me to a closed hamlet
called Stuck.
I lifted my eyes
to The Present Strength.
True mercy comes
to those who accept it
without burdening themselves,
feeling unworthy of love.
Why waste strength demanding
what is freely given?

Why refuse what the Holy One
shares mercifully?
Most likely to mislead me
is the hardening of my own heart.
In a spirit of peace
I will begin again,
stepping as I am led.
I will trust the Holy One
to dry a pathway
between threatening waves
of greed and envy.

Psalm 45

IN THE QUIET of night You visit,
finding me unable to sleep.
The weight of professional
and personal problems
combine to feel like tons.
Lost at a crossroads,
I call on You.
Help me refuse to choose
by degree of difficulty
and accept when the best stance
may be urgent flight.
Joy is reflecting
on making the right decision
even when the choice leads
to pain or loss of face.

Although I tremble,
I enter the fray.
I am confident
that each new step will bring
renewed courage.
Should I reach the end
of my endurance,
my faith declares that
Your updraft will always
carry me closer
to a major prize
that may be won
by my descendants.

Psalm 46

AS A MOTHER pushes
through childbirth's pain,
I push through setbacks.
Rising, I glorify
Your magnificence.
The fullness of Your love
facilitates trust
that sincere homage
will outweigh the defects
in my offerings.
The distance between
my beginning and this day
is insignificant
when measured against
Your Holy existence.
Fully adult, I acknowledge
You as my master.

Psalm 47

THE ILLUSION is sun falling
splash-free into the water.
There is no solar plunge,
only a continuing revolution
of another lesser being.
We Your children
also do not fall
when we choose to rise
again in service,
and take heart because
You have blessed us to stand.
May we prove ourselves
worthy of a million rebirths,
each baptism sweeter
than the one that preceded.
Each rise another night break.

Psalm 48

IN THE WORSHIP assembly
are those who have no intention
of praising You for their blessings.
They consider themselves
too sophisticated
and far too deserving
to offer holy adoration.
Help them honor their gifts.
Let the whitened glare
of modern deeds not obscure
the velvety Light
of modern faithfulness.
All glory be directed to You
whom distractions
cannot overpower.

77

Psalm 49

WHEN the fishing village
is transformed
into a playground
for the well-to-do,
the ghetto becomes
a white-collar refuge,
and the family farm
is purchased for getaways,
where do the people run
if not to You?
Does the meaning
of justice change
when the lines are drawn
with dollar signs?

What is love's meaning
when the question itself
is deemed irrelevant?
Help us to frame queries
so that modern pharaohs
and the new Pilates
will not pontificate
on market demands.
Soften their hard hearts.
Surely they understand
we cannot make bricks
when we are denied
essential elements,
and that slavery
by any other name
is foe to justice.

Psalm 50

YOU KNOW ALL TOO WELL

my time on this earth

has caused me to forget

what should always

be remembered.

Once upon a time

I let myself cry

loud enough to be heard.

May my own soul be touched

as I come to a child

in the midst of screaming.

It is not my calling

to stand as maestro

conducting the music

of babies' cries.

May I set aside
the will to dominate
and help the child find
a place of comfort.
May the song I sing
begin in my heart
and move to my hands,
bringing compassion
through all life's stages.
May I soothe by loving,
improvise with tenderness,
step beyond bloodlines,
and sing as though I am
the angel of love.

Psalm 51

YOU ARE THE ONE
who remains through all losses.
I weigh myself and find
that once upon a time
I defined myself as
son, grandson, and nephew.
On both sides of my family,
each who empowered
the words is dead.
I still live in countless circles:
by gender and race,
social class and politics,
religion and birthplace,
skills and interests.

Then there is You,
the only One who
is never a foreigner.
Speaking all languages,
even those that omit words,
Your unity awes.
I am pushing myself
to expand identity
from desire to am.
Restrain my practice
from othering anyone.
Help me to sing songs
more closely aligned with Yours.

Psalm 52

WHILE SINGING peace songs
for our Great Parent,
the lyrics change
from person to person
and moment to moment.
Grace rains like spring showers.
This soil is too moist
for the desert to own,
too multi-lingual
for any country to claim.
We hear rhythm kept
by a trillion drummers.
Dazzling music is sung
by those who fear crowds
and those who fear solitude.

The melodies echo
from the farm to city.
The piano, saxophones, and trumpets
mix with a bass line
steadily pushing the world.
Together we praise You
for the care and visitations
you make to the needy.
The peace song is You,
and we are Yours.
Out of the chaos
into compassion.

Psalm 53

THE MOST POWERFUL temptation
is to seek Your face
only in our spare time,
or on a set-aside day.
The second is to use reluctance to criticize
as a shield for what is unacceptable.
Through cowardice,
we license destroyers
while maintaining our own clear conscience.
Let us open our hearts first to You
and then to our neighbors.
In sustaining this willingness to serve,
we will not lose sight
of the pain we inflict.

Moreover, we will be able to find joy
even as we absorb
the sufferers' despair.
Compassion is the ladder
from the snake pit,
where suggestions are hissed
that we take bites from
the tree of exploitation.
Draw us steadily to the One
who moves from strength to strength.

88

Psalm 54

YOUR HOLY ARMS are like smoke
curling from a lonely prairie house,
offering welcome on a frigid day.
In the midst of my solitary trek,
I enter Your sanctuary.
Already heads are bowed
in praise and supplication.
The wise have heard Your request
as a command to leave busyness
and enter a place of peace,
where we will be in the presence
of the One Who Listens.
Help us to distinguish Your will
from too-fertile imaginations.
Should we err, may we do so
always on the side of kindness.
When I leave my kin in faith,
I return to a cold world
where some are fortified with nothing
and we are strengthened by Your being.

Psalm 55

WHEN WILL my sorrow end?
Must I carry it into the next world?
Lamenting, I turn to You, knowing
foolishly I have brought
deep grief's weight upon myself.
Forgive me my failure
to heed Your warnings.
Looking back I see clearly
how I deceived myself.
The highway filled
with bells and whistles
was far from the right path.
Ambition should never have driven me.
Where I know less
than I think I know,
clarify my ignorance
that I may not mislead my neighbor.
Where I know more
than I think I know,
help me honor my intuition
and stride forward, spreading truth.

Psalm 56

THE FOOL ASKS, "How many times must I
remake myself after breaks?"
The wise sing, "Once more with feeling."
Help us mine yesterday's errors
for the golden nuggets
with which we may purchase
a shiny tomorrow.
Help us prove ourselves
exemplary in each assignment.
Increase our dignity whether
we select the struggle or stumble
into the fray.

Make us merchants who
both purchase and offer Truth
at wholesale prices.
Make us justice farmers
who sow equity in this life
instead of status mongers
who tell people
it is best to wait
for pie in the sky
in the next.

Psalm 57

BY YOUR COMMAND,
we are the rebels
who refuse to collapse
into the arms
of overindulgence.
Simplifying our possessions
to redistribute for the needy,
we offer our devotion
to the One,
not the many gods.
Shiny idols are presented
in the guise
of greed and comfort.
In measured love-strides,
we move toward our siblings
left on society's fringes.
With joyful adoration for You,
we smile each mile
that we travel the race course
designed by the Giver of Love.

Psalm 58

MOVING TOWARD RECONCILIATION,

years after the stabbings,
my back is almost healed.
I sing as a survivor.
Thank You for being patient
with my weakness
as I carried a weight
that tempered my joy much too long.
Instead of searching for revenge,
it is healthier to forgive
myself for trusting the unworthy.
It is possible to abandon bitterness,
and strip the forces of division
of their fearsome power.
Together we have the ability
to heal much of the world.

Psalm 59

BESIDE a great lake,
sharing the dawn with You,
I see the sun appear to rise
through the water.
So it is with my soul
when I leave a dry spell
and reunite
with Your ever-constant love.
Each moment's warmth
evokes the feeling
of an eternal embrace.
Joy is my awareness of You,
and knowing that I make myself useful
by serving Your world.
Leaving my island,
I am swept up in awe
of ten thousand sunrises
slept through in one thousand places.

Psalm 60

IN THE COOLNESS
of a summer evening,
the road leads to You,
even as it has through
all other weathers.
Grace should be treasured.
Nothing is more ungrateful
than looking past
Your compassion.
We reflect back
on how many times
You have rescued our souls
and fed our needs.
Thank You for all
that makes us worthy
to be called Your children.

Psalm 61

LET THE GOVERNMENT soldier remember
the ones who gave love.
Let the spiritual soldier remember
the call to give love.
If single-focus
and unquestioning obedience
is the quest's design,
let us choose wisely
whom we shall serve.
Some say, "Twenty years and out."
Those who volunteer
to fight on Your side
have a lifelong term
with furloughs only for sleeping,
a time when dreams should be
of a better, shared tomorrow.
Let us accept our private's rank
without striving
to give our own orders.
Let us count
all victories as Yours,
not our own.

Psalm 62

MANY of my neighbors
consider appreciation of Your love
to be superstition
if not madness.
Limiting my respect
to frail humans
is not enough for me.
Down here on the ground, covered
by a deceptively clear winter sky,
I savor my numerous blessings,
then move toward Truth.
May the spirits of deceased loved ones
dwell in eternity:
part of the choosers
who chose to be chosen.
May my descendants
carry onward the sweetness
of my recollections.
May their pursuit bring
a world of glittering compassion.

Psalm 63

THE HOLY ONE,
who alone dwells in perfection,
favors those denied choice.
A newborn chooses
neither health nor race,
gender nor country,
social nor economic class.
Innocence ensures
the infant is highly favored.
We cannot measure the purpose
in what appears,
to our limited vision,
to be no more than accident.

Adults who lack the power
to control outcomes
also have You as Protector.
Help the slave, whether confined
to a plantation or a prison.
Help the person needing work
that will feed, house, clothe,
and educate a family.
Keep hope alive
and make opportunity real.

Psalm 64

SEEKING EXPERIENCES

that sweep the corners
clean of corruption,
we turn to You,
our spiritual GPS.
Although self-purification
is out of reach,
You accept us.
We are not content
with our own shortcomings.
Our commitment
to staying the course
that leads to justice
is what separates
us from the whiners and the posers.
We understand that our passionate demands
rile the powerful.
Forgive us when our best is misguided.
Prod us when our truce is mistimed.
Bless us when our cause is just.

Psalm 65

I PLACE MY FAITH in You,
not in how the interpreters
try to define You, confine You.
On stained-glass and in pictures
they transform the Son's
desert-tanned being
into blond hair and blue eyes.
When asked the purpose of the pictures,
they say the portraits are prayer aids.
Could it be they believe
we are not wise enough
to realize You are the Great Spirit,
not created in their image?

Your majesty is limitless.
How can anyone paint You
and claim honesty?
What can we say of You
that will define Your will?
How can we obsess on yesteryear
while knowing that
time has no meaning
to the Alpha and Omega?
You, without our aid, created the first.
Should we destroy the world,
You will outlive the last.

Psalm 66

YOUR BLUE JAYS FLIT from back to front
and then back again,
before crossing into the yard
to which our neighbor has a deed.
Jays ignore boundaries drawn eons after
You gave their ancestors this land.
Their inner compasses remain attuned
to the world You created.
I ask my soul
to rise and fly.
This is the day that you have made
without carving it into pieces.

May we strive to sustain it
in the face of enslavements,
underpayments and devaluations,
bombs, drones, and missiles,
holocausts and genocides,
though many glorify
the perpetrators
as though oppression
can be a work of beauty.
May we be the jays who fly
above counterfeit boundaries
carved by earthly surveyors.

106

Psalm 67

SEND SPIRITUAL SOLACE
as solid as redwoods
standing in virgin forests.
Sweep the swells
from beneath salty eyes.
Let them see that
Victory is Your name.
The colors have faded
from bright to sepia.
The memories of the pits
from which you rescued us—
slaves in Georgia and Mississippi,
dismayed in Virginia and Alabama,
persecuted in Ohio and New York—
are brought into the light.
The origin of their illumination
is Your steadfast mercy.
You are the Holy One
who never leaves the captives forlorn.
All praise to Your freeing power.
May we continue what You have begun.

Psalm 68

I HAVE ARRIVED at the appointed hour
only to wait
for those scheduled to meet me.
Sometimes my greeter has expected
someone of another race,
or much older,
claimed to be held up in traffic,
or to have fallen asleep.
I am not an innocent.
Only You can count
the many times I have failed
to answer Your call.
In the midst of reflection,
I close my eyes
and sense Your smiling spirit.
Forgive my self-righteous impatience.
Accept my sincere intention
to be at Your service
in all seasons and
at Your chosen hour.

Psalm 69

STEPPING AWAY from busyness
I quiet myself and wait
to hear Your voice.
Forgive me
for allowing righteous anger
to invite distractions.
Clarity is within reach.
Blessed be the one who remembers
that disciplining oneself
is a step toward being healed.
May I be
a never-collapsing bridge.
May I bring
together disparate parts
in a unity held together
by Your magnificence.

Psalm 70

TOGETHER we make this stand
although the world expects us
to be crushed like ants
under oversized shoes.
We carry no arms beyond Truth,
but Truth cannot be vanquished
by the world's weapons.
I look up and down the line.
Your Light shines within
every woman, man, and child.
There has never been a day like today.
We rise with the wings of eagles.
Under Your banner we cannot fail.
Forward!
Should we link with You,
justice is assured.

Psalm 71

FEARLESSLY I ask evil
to get behind me.
Follow if you dare.
I am walking
in the Lord's steps.
My destination is the city
of Holy Obedience.
Where I go,
you will be transformed.

Psalm 72

SOME TAKE YOUR LOVE for granted
because of a covenant
they say You made with ancestors.
No one speaks of an escape clause.
How many times have we failed
to hold up our part
of the bargain?
The only thing that could keep it binding
is Your unending forgiveness.
We apologize
for a billion breaches.
We have preferred war to negotiation.
We have chosen hatred over acceptance.
We have built walls of separation.
Grant us wisdom that can sustain
peace for more than a moment
and love that stretches across all lines.

Psalm 73

THE MISGUIDED ask me to suffer
while they live in luxury.
You, the One I worship,
encourage me forward.
I do not flinch
at the price
of Holy Obedience.
If social justice demands anything,
its highest price is less
than the price
for being an oppressor.

Psalm 74

SILK-LIKE comfort sifts
through silent prayer.
Softness evaporates in the wind.
You are sending me
to meet face-to-face
with the abandoned.
You are not the god of comfort.
You are the Deity of Comforting.
When it pleases,
You say, "Go,"
with a flatness
pregnant with love.

Armed only with faith,
I face weapon-carrying tormentors.
Yours is the mission.
Whom shall I fear?
As caregiver, I am consoled
with a healing
straight from Your being.
Thank You
for Your bluntness
with one so stubborn
as sometimes to question
both You and those Hell-bent
on blocking progress.

Psalm 75

SOME SPEAK of being saved.
I ask: For what? From what? To what?
Enslaved, my ancestors
cried out to You
for deliverance
from bondage.
They desired the ability
to choose something
other than life or death.
Even when few loved us,
You made jagged lines
into recognizable circles.
Wholeness is Your passion,
a space beyond our understanding,
a civilization that brooks
no decadence,
a time that knows
no end.

117

Psalm 76

DEEP INSIDE WINTER,
I learned to love browns
in all their many forms,
the trees bare
except for squirrel nests,
the grass almost as dry
as potato chips,
my neighbors struggling to believe
in a spring of any sort.
I pray that the lure
of green never blinds me
to opportunity hanging
as low as ripe fruit.

May my attention always be drawn
to the greatest
of possibilities
instead of being immobilized
by what is denied.
Help me to empower others
to embrace the vibrancy
of the same browns
that I once easily dismissed
as lacking beauty and symbolizing death.
All the while they were
new beginning's promise.

Psalm 77

ONCE MORE I have learned
of a baby whose life
has been ravaged
by heart disease.
These special angels
are precious to You.
May I never turn my back
on the pain of those
for whom we are called to care.
The mystery of death
complicates my acts
when the deceased life
lasts but a moment.

It is impossible to demonstrate
my own children deserved
to be born healthy.
Take my life, it is Yours.
Use it in service
to babies struggling
against all odds
and the supporting parents.
Bring your healing
and let us honor
the deaths of these heroes
by earning the right
to be listed among
Your ambassadors.

Psalm 78

MY SIBLINGS SHIVER
as though standing in a blizzard
waiting for an overdue bus.
Warmth is available inside,
away from fire-eating dragons
and crazed unicorns
that we are told do not exist.
You will not come
in the form of a phoenix.
You have no need
to rise from the ashes
for You have never fallen.
In this hour of need
inject Your strength.
The wait is over
when the will is present.
This is the day that
You have made.
In full power
we hold the line.

Psalm 79

WE APPROACH YOU,

the Blameless One.
Although we offer
an assortment of disabilities—
physical, mental,
spiritual, and emotional—
we offer the best of ourselves.
Some disabilities we have inherited.
Others were forced upon us.
Forgive us the ones
that are conquerable
but that we choose to nurture.

Help us avoid cursing
the ones which are beyond
our capacity to change.
Let impairments
never create distance.
We trust You
never to forsake us.
Simultaneously we confess
that sometimes we have turned
our backs on You.
In our shallowness
increase our depth,
for Yours is the ownership
now and throughout eternity.

Psalm 80

MISSING REALITY,
the painter attempts
to capture a vista.
Constantly we overlook
details in Your creation.
And yet the climb from the floor
is worth the journey
when done honorably.
Denying opportunity
to those below water level
rarely has anything to do with merit.
Justice has an Edenic view.
Have I searched for beauty
and contented myself with excess?

Have I searched for power
and refused to use it
for the betterment
of the oppressed?
Forgive me my myopia.
Sweep away my delusions.
Let me fly to You and Yours.
Though I travel a little
slower than an angel,
may my route be equally direct.

Psalm 81

I COME to the stream's branch;
unsure of my next stroke,
I cry, "Lord, have mercy.
Please guide this canoe
in the right direction."
The land appears wild and virgin.
I am a reluctant frontiersman.
I want to dodge ice floes,
push away floating timbers.
Will the ones beside me bail out
from the next threat?
Does it matter when
I can always count on You?
I continue singing the voyageur's song,
paddling with gusto,
preparing for possibilities
beyond my control,
but always under
Your authority.

Psalm 82

YOUR WORLD is not about
individuals acting
in imitation
of immature gods,
ordering the poor about.
The command is to pool
the best of our love.
We bring our own instruments,
but not to perform in solitude.
Compositions we
have been called to play
are written by Your hand.

Forgive us the murders,
sexual assaults,
and embezzlements,
committed by neighbors
whom we should have helped
understand that oppression
is the seed of violence.

Forgive us the isolation
we have thrust upon too many.

If we have done anything
to enable any abuse or loneliness,
forgive us for the
accomplices we became.

Psalm 83

I HEARD Your voice
as I sat inside
my loneliness.
You reminded me
I was not alone.
From being divided
from my courage,
I found my own powerful voice.
You are not a green leaf
blown by the slightest breeze.
You are the untamed wind itself.
In finding my original wildness,
I reunited with the One.

Psalm 84

OUR IDENTITY does not change
with place of residence
or as an overawed tourist.
By remembering who owns it all
wherever we roam
we are world citizens.
Thank You
for giving us a loving home.
We are Your followers,
Your servants,
Your children.
Let us honor Your creation
in its fullness.

Psalm 85

MY EYES REST
on the screen;
I see a disfigured man.
I wonder if our stories
are linked in any way.
Did I send him off to war
in search of oil
or fail to hear You say,
"Your brother is in need?"
In the next scene sits
a woman with a contorted face.
Did I help poison my sister
with pollution
that I failed to prevent?
Who am I if Your children
suffer at my neglect?
How can I be untainted
if I pretend not to hear You call?

Psalm 86

IN A LOVER'S TOUCH

is the same endless possibility
as the breath You share
with a newborn.
You are the thread who stitches
pieces into one purity.
Help me recall that
once I knew no fears
and my love was without restraints.
Release me to live
in endless spring,
not because winter is absent,
but because blossoming is perpetual.

Psalm 87

I APPEAL TO YOU
for I am floundering.
They do not understand
misuse is abuse.
Because it has been a part
of our country for so long,
the majority look past it.
Like a splinter
floating away
from a sinking ship,
I watch the gulf widen.
The victims of bias are blamed
for their own oppression.
Meanwhile the users
smile on magazine covers,
laugh on talk shows,
and say, "Send them back,"

as though they are originals
who never left the Rift Valley.

I beg You to save us
from the type of rage
that erupts into self-destruction.
Fueled by Your love,
teach us impatient patience
and patient impatience.
Sustain our determination
when we are tempted
to believe acceptance
is the only way to remain sane.
Let blue songs and laughter
shape our energy
into the ability
to build a just world.

Psalm 88

ABOVE MY HEAD I hear
periodic planes slicing lines
through the night sky.
Down here, sick and confined
to a bed not of my choice,
I feel like a merchant waylaid
by a highway robber who says,
"Your money or your life."
This thief makes it clear,
both might be forfeited
without pricking
the brigand's conscience.
I will not tremble
while in Your company.
Compassionate One,
I know the sky
is not falling.
My spirit will rise to greet
the new dawn in all its fullness.

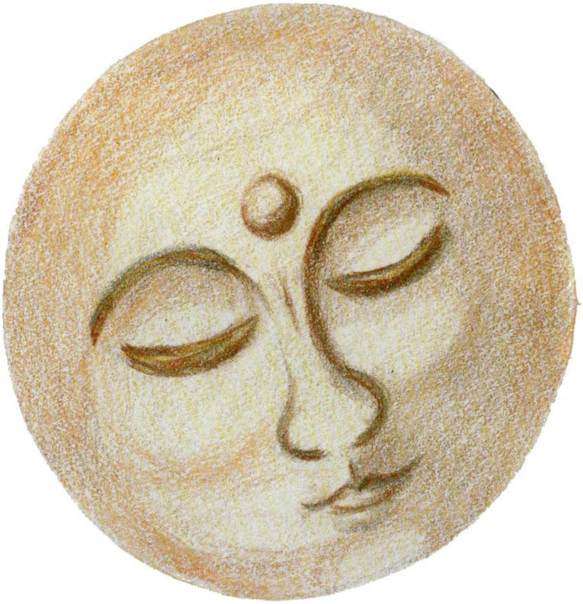

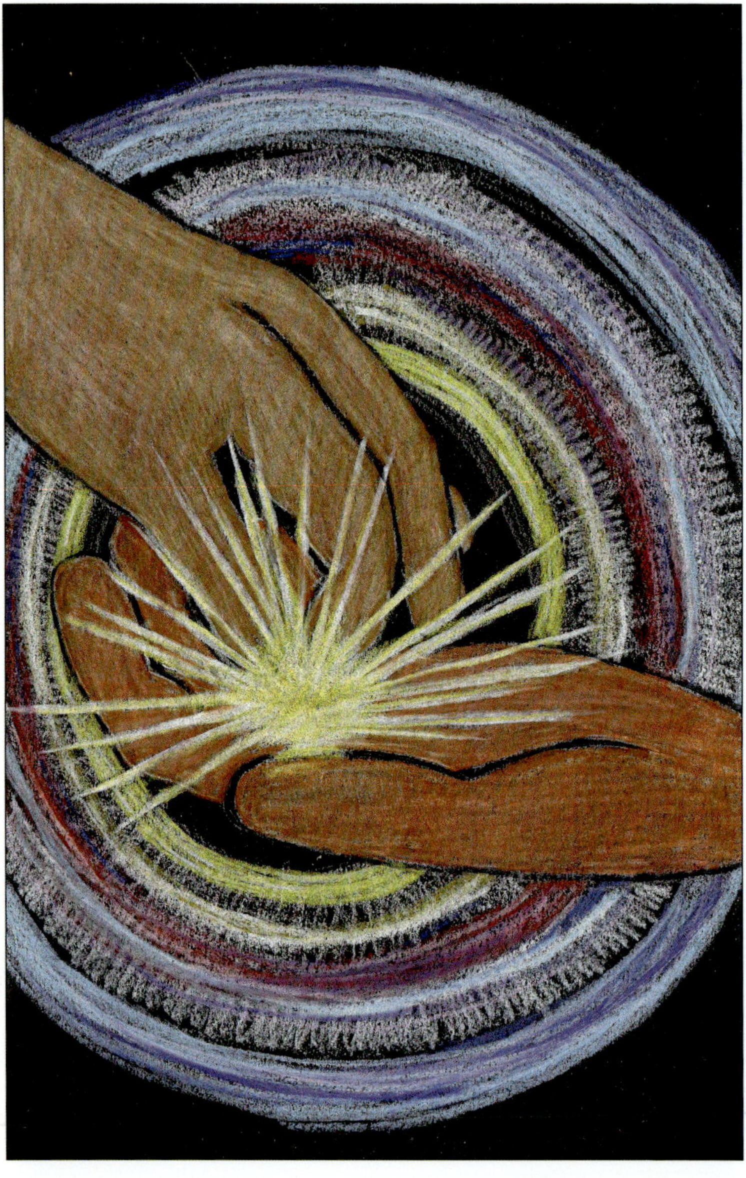

Psalm 89

I PRAY FOR my siblings
with mental and emotional illnesses
who have been tossed into streets
by those with hardened hearts.
Ejected, rejected, and dejected,
they are in need of mercy.
Help us make love live
by singing Your song
of the extended hand.
Passionate compassion
brings peace of mind
to the whole body.
Benign neglect chokes
the soul of one
while stunting the growth of both.

Psalm 90

IN YOUR NAME, my hand
has been extended
to the homebound.
I have written letters,
cards, and emails.
I have come to their doors
bearing food and drink.
I have sat in their living rooms
holding conversations
about our personal joys and sorrows.
As death approached,
I have prayed at their bedsides,
and tutored their children.

The thought of leaving this life
frightens some and relieves others.
Following the rainbow
to its natural end
is inescapable.
May I always
bring my best energy
to these, Your children.
Help us appreciate
Your colors as radiating hope
and leave this our present life
with dignity intact.

Psalm 91

ON A COLD and rainy day
I looked deeply into
a homeless woman's eyes.
Surprised that a giver
recognized her humanity,
she hugged me.
Had I offered Your child
ten dollars, five, or maybe a single?
All I recall is her response
was more to my
open acceptance
than to the number on the bill.
And You were there.
Her eyes had taken on an
unmistakable new light.

Forgive me
for the many times
that I have given a part of my heart
and none of my eyes.
Help me remember
Your song falls flat
when singers only go
through the motions,
as if wishing someone would disappear
both from sight and possibility.
I am not called to save the world,
but I am called to be real
with those whose paths I cross.

Psalm 92

WE ARE A CHOIR

whose song never ends.
We live in freshness,
climbing unseen heights
despite attempts
to prevent our singing.
In a voice
that is not our own,
serenading possibilities,
making them reality.
In tribute to Your
everlasting glory,
we begin Your composition
on our knees.

In the fullness of time
we stand and walk.
Humbly we acknowledge
that we are the people
whose victory is made of peace
and whose reason for existing
is to serve.

Psalm 93

WITHOUT FEAR of slipping,
Your invisible servants, the Angels,
skip on icy grounds
where no trail is nor ever was.
At times we have suffered mightily.
Throughout our period on earth,
we, Your ordinary people,
have been rescued
when it seemed we were
on the point of annihilation.
Always we have risen gloriously,
stepping in the footsteps
of the angels.

Thank You for our heroic ancestors.
We especially honor
those who acted
against their previous high stories,
surprising many
by uncovering
their true greatness.
We are peacemaking soldiers,
carrying weapons of construction,
led by a tri-colored flag beaming
love, unity, compassion.

Psalm 94

I HAVE WALKED with foster children
who go from house to house
looking for a home,
often feeling unloved
by anyone but You.
I have visited the homes
of the impoverished
who were embarrassed
for me to see conditions
that once upon a time
I knew too well.
These are not the only ones
who comb this life seeking welcome.
We beg for mercy in myriad ways.
Help the ones called
to offer mercy, give mercy.
Only You can offer absolution
for the times when one is called
yet deliberately looks in another direction.
Help us see in detail
all that we are tempted to scan.

149

Psalm 95

THE HOLY SPIRIT

gently tugs my sleeve.

She knows I've volunteered

to follow the Good Shepherd's

directions. Lead me

with Your superior knowledge.

Accept my whispered praises

and my actions designed

to move society

toward justice.

Help me rise,

mind stayed on You,

clear, clean, and claiming.

Psalm 96

IN AN HOUR of need,
when I was too young to pray,
and poverty had me down,
Your compassionate arms
rescued my family
from the cold.
What I do in maturity,
I do for love,
not in a vain attempt
to reimburse You.
Some debts are too large
to kid oneself
about ever fully repaying.

Accept my offering
as simply as I bring it,
with mature strength
as well as trepidation.
Though it is a mere shadow
compared to Your largesse,
I give freely even as I received,
with the hope that it makes
a positive difference
in the search
for peace and justice.

Psalm 97

OUR PARENT who exists
beyond and within,
Yours is the greatest identity.
Your earthly vision
become reality.
Your pleasure
become our acts.
Sustain us
with what is necessary.
Forgive us our debts to You
in equal measure
as we show mercy to strangers.
Make us aware
of our weaknesses,
and sufficiently courageous
to overcome them.
Yours is the earth and all its riches,
the only power and majesty
that we honor as above ourselves.

Psalm 98

OFTEN WE DISAGREE with lyrics
because our experience
does not match the composer's.
Sustain our faith
despite our disappointments.
Life must be measured
not merely through our own lens.
Our neighbors' treatment
is also our concern.
To blame a newborn
with health issues,
or see You as disloyal
for any innocent's woes,
is shortsighted finger-pointing.

Some parents
of chronically ill children
make themselves instruments
of healing
for countless others.
Lessons learned from lost prizes
benefit those who follow.
When I would make
premature pronouncements,
help me hold my peace
until the stillness
becomes clarity.

Psalm 99

YOU ARE a spirited Spirit.
Your essence is love and compassion.
You flow like a pristine river,
rising like a justice tide,
overflowing like a parent's love
for the returning prodigal.
Shall we dance the night away,
or concentrate on silently walking
together along the stream?
Wherever You lead,
we will know You by Your healing.

Psalm 100

I AM FOREVER an initiate
being introduced
into Your special society.
Help me bear witness
as a man of courage,
following the lead
of the Master.
Thank You
for not hazing me
when I lose my way home.

Nothing stays the same as it was.
I have never been
in this present moment.
You have been and are everywhere.
Lead.
Make me the human
You intended.

Psalm 101

WITH TONGUE in cheek,
You ordered physicians
to first heal themselves.
We are incapable
of healing anyone
without Your assistance.
For our part,
fools focus on themselves
even as the wise study You.
I see my temptations.
They walk boldly,
barefoot over pointed nails or,
on formal days, in wooden clogs,
clomping loudly with each step.

They act like commanding officers
determined to be saluted on sight.
When they are tamed,
it is by appealing
to Your strength.
You are the One
who restrains these bullies.
Thank You for Your patience
with my wayward soul.

Psalm 102

TOGETHER YOU AND I travel city streets
and the few remaining meadows
where loved ones who will never return,
laughed, cried, and sang.
I am in mourning,
yet I am energized
by these living spaces
as I can be by no traditional cemetery.
You brought these special guests into my life
and ensure that
fragrant memories linger.
Even in my longing,
loneliness is absent.

Loosened pains
cross the sky like geese
flying in V-formation
off to new adventures.
I savor the unspoken promise of return.
You ensure that sting
is accompanied by victory.
This is my inland island,
the cherished spot
on a dreamer's map.
Blessed was I.
Blessed am I.

Psalm 103

THE DESERT is not always
a place of sand and high heat.
We seek an oasis in a temperate climate.
The quest is for the promised land.
Our work is an extension
of labor begun generations earlier,
increasing its value.
Our sweat most often is caused
by injustices masked as fairness.
Your love is always manna,
the undeserved, sustaining present
when we are on the verge of faltering.
Help us withstand the counsel of fools
and the temptation of idols.
Help us understand that
we are never powerless.

Psalm 104

IN THE SHADOW of steeples
purportedly dedicated to You,
they monger fear
and victimize the outcasts.
We are one in the Spirit
although divided in narratives.
Help those who claim
to have accepted
the universal call
to love one another.
Honoring life includes restoration
of scandalized reputations
as well as destroyed lands.
May we imagine
in our songs of unity
Eden's splendor returned.

Psalm 105

THE POOR SEEK their allotted portion,
certain that You do not choose
to leave them standing
cold and empty handed.
Is their justice
to be denied forever?
Must they wait on crumbs
to trickle down
from the overloaded tables
of those who consume lives?
Self-anointed prophets say
that you promise,
"I will grant your desire
if you shall not be moved."
Who anointed those claiming
to speak in Your name?
So often they join in the fleecing.
Surely Your beloved
are more than sheep

assigned to wear thin polyester
while their leaders
wear tailored merino suits.
Surely we were not made
to be easily misled
by mimickers of empathy.
Is there balm in the slums
as well as in Gilead?
Can solace be found
on reservations and in barrios?
Help us arm with peaceful resolve,
never resorting to weapons.
What can be sustained requires love.
Help us avoid apathy,
the most common
killer of victory.
While our strength still flowers,
let the fruit of the tree of life
visit our homes.

Psalm 106

OUR COUNTRY 'tis of Thee.
May we pledge it to liberty's pursuit.
When we lift our voices and sing,
may our appeal be to the One
who brooks no divisions.
Your creation's design was awe-filled.
May we restore it to goodness.
Supreme love is the binder
that perfects the vision and
swells peace from sea to sea.

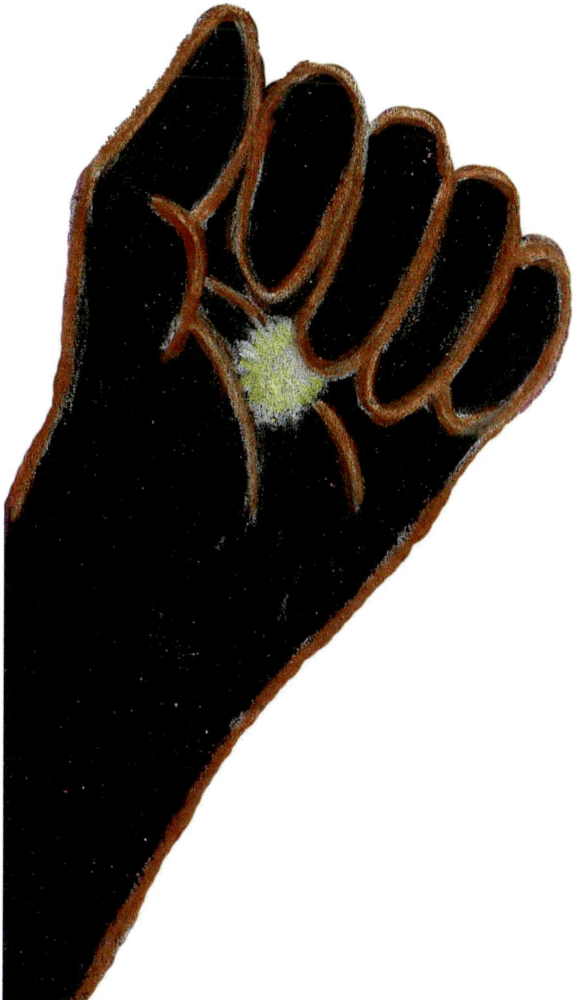

Psalm 107

TRUE PROTECTION
is only found in You.
The need for parenting
outlasts one's youth.
We ask You
to make Your presence known
to the parents who cannot parent:
the ones who were too deeply wounded
in their own youth
to rise to wholeness;
the ones who have lost
the only child they will ever have;
the ones whose children push them away,
or were taken by another;
the ones who are in prison
or on jobs that take them off;
the ones who wanted to parent

but never found a dream-maker lover;
the ones prevented by a disability;
the ones who regret a youthful decision
that denied a life;
the ones who lost
a never-forgotten child
before, during, or after birth;
the ones whose abuses prevented growth.
You are the Great Parent
of us all.
Help us remember
the absent presences,
and channel our love
toward all the orphans, castoffs,
relatives, and others who could benefit
from untapped love.

Psalm 108

I WOULD HAVE been content
to swim in blues but
You brought azure, cerulean, and lapis lazuli.
You said, "There is more to pain
than meets the heart.
Suffering is no guarantee of closeness."
You taught me hope
and provided opportunity.
I am the one you rescued
with the kindness
that is Your nature.
I sing Your praises
even as the summer breeze
makes music as it passes through
ancient chimes
that have been weathered
by sun, rains, and snow.

171

Psalm 109

YOU ARE MY PROTECTOR.
I am tempted by no other.
Although I walk through
the killing fields of America
where I may be bloodied on sidewalks,
in schools or malls,
churches or theaters,
I will fear no evil.
Your love and Your compassion
are my constant companions,
identical twins birthed by the same Parent.

You prepare wholesome food
and untainted water
for my sustenance.
From this home,
I shall never be evicted.
Lead me to the pristine streams
of Your desire.
When I am tempted to be strategic,
or to accept the counsel of the selfish,
help me remember that my heart
should only bow to Your will.

Psalm 110

THE LORD is with me
in this cold rain.
Despite the lowering temperature,
I move forward, head bowed.
Had I left when called, I'd be home.
There will be no looking back with longing,
regretting the loss
of ground already overcome.
You are my Promise
as You were my Deliverer.
Forgive my earlier hesitations.
The delay was not
through lack of faith in You.
I wallowed in my own unworthiness
not realizing it was never about me.
The power was always Yours
to dispense as You choose.

Psalm 111

LIKE BIRDS SHELTERING

from autumn rain,
we seek Your grace
from hateful attacks.
They come for us although
we are not even bystanders.
They stigmatize us
with their bigotry.
Words of hatred are delivered
in Your name
despite knowing
you demand compassion.
We are lost
without your divine shield.
Help us stand tall,
calling on Your name,
not resorting to the same hatred
as those who torment us willingly.
We have dedicated our lives
to Your service.
We shall not be turned around.

Psalm 112

WANDERING through wilderness,
I have often wondered
when will I know
Your presence again?
But I cause this lusterless
loneliness, I block the reunion.
You are always available.
Forgive me my pride as I hold
onto guilt and rage, shame and stubbornness.
No one said, "Trust me."
I have betrayed myself.
Sweet Sovereign, may I,
in all ways, prove less a fool
and more Your intended.
Wholeness is only my bowed head away.

Psalm 113

ON A STREET FILLED
with stretch limousines,
and expensive aromas
from gourmet restaurants,
the castoffs panhandle
until the police tell them
to move along far from sight.
To be an inconvenience
for those with every convenience
is a humbling thing.
To be loved only
by You is not a curse.
Teach us to value ourselves
even when our neighbors
disdain our presence.
Keep us from accepting
the disrespect of puffy clouds
and help us
to build our foundation
on the solid Rock
that is Your being.

Psalm 114

IN THE DISTANCE a rainbow
arches far from our neighborhood.
Here a throwaway nation lives
removed from prosperity.
Your children are living parallel lives.
Lift Your gracious voice
to teach the peacemakers
a new song
taking them from pews and electronic screens
into the streets
where the stuff that breaks wills
runs roughshod over dreams.
Let them learn that the one to glorify
is not the crumb-giver who trumpets greed.
We sing of the generous who invite all
to the first setting
of Your banquet table.
You are the bringer
of opportunities,
the insurer
of life beyond fluff.

Psalm 115

YOUR SONG COMES without vibrato,
vibrating my heart.
Your song comes with vibrato,
stilling my heart.
It is not the tone or pitch that matters.
What matters is that
it is Your song,
and not theirs or even mine.
Blessed is the community
that never attempts
to drown Your voice,
the one that understands
we are backups
and not star attractions.
I thrill to Your music, snap my fingers,
and move my feet.
In ecstasy, I whirl and step,
losing myself as I find myself,
swept up in Your love.

Psalm 116

FROM THE DAWN of time in Africa,
we sang songs to You.
We lost our language
along with our freedom,
our connection to our ancestors,
and the land we held sacred.
Kidnapping and slavery
changed none of our devotion
to You, or our love of justice.
In anguish we toiled unpaid
for the good of others.
You are the Inalienable Truth,
the One who paves all roads
leading away from oppression.
May we never forget the travails
of previous generations
and that You remain our Redeemer.

Psalm 117

I WONDER HOW spring jumped to winter.
You overawe each time I pause
to consider what is unfolding
before my eyes.
The song You sing is mystifying.
From the distance
I see skyscrapers.
They cannot dwarf the sea,
nor shield far off mountains.
Your natural world feeds
my imagination, growing my soul,
and circling me back
to Eternal Newness.

Psalm 118

IGNORING our common origin,
they told me to draw lines
and call them races.
Without consulting those present
before their arrival,
they called other lines borders.
If asked, "Is this God-ordained?"
they always use actions to say,
"You superstitious fools,
there is no unseen God.
There is only the physical currency
which we worship
and designate our sovereign."
In this foreign land
which is my birthplace,
shield us from detours to Truth.
Help us pledge our allegiance
to the One who circles all.

Psalm 119

THE DAY is sunny,
but rain is on my mind.
I know my Redeemer lives.
I offer a token purchased long ago
on another toll road.
I know my Redeemer lives.
You accept my contribution.
Always and forever,
I sing of endless possibilities.
Thank you for washed-away sorrow,
and the courage to believe
when a million shakedown ministers
make a mockery of Your majesty.
I know my Redeemer lives
though all around me are doubters.
I know my Redeemer lives,
Your mighty love a continuing
crescendo of compassion,
moving across my memory,
empowering me
in this sustained moment.
I know my Redeemer lives.

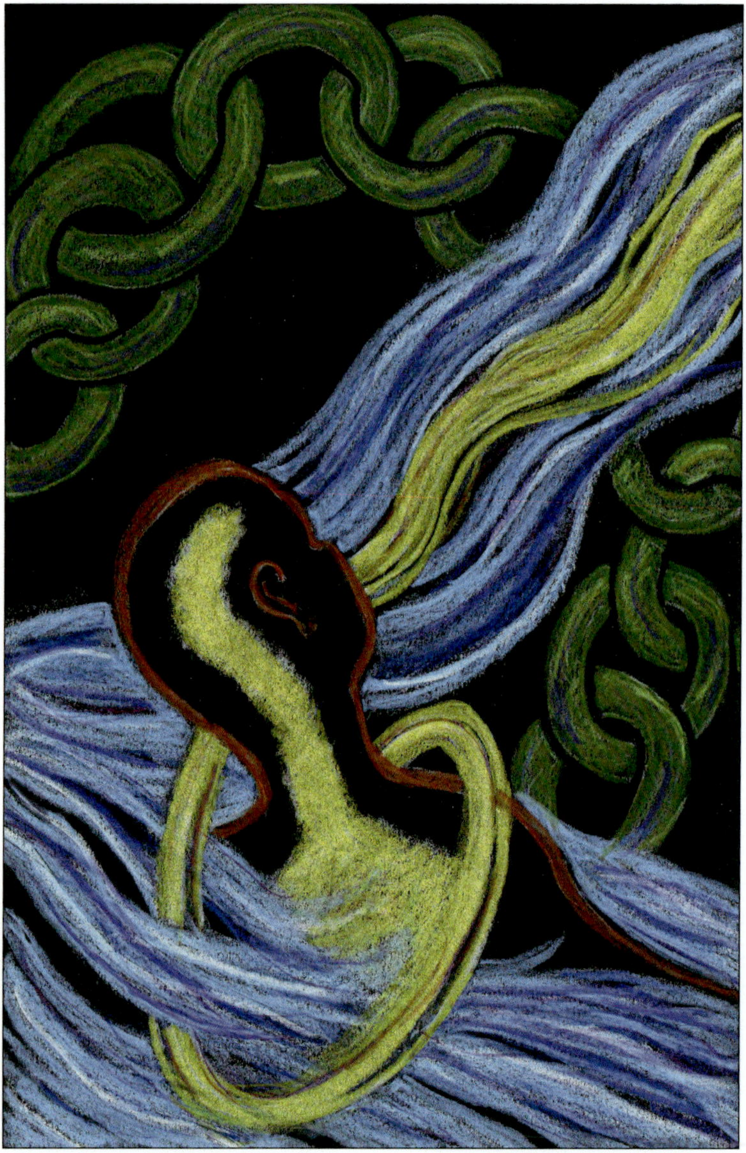

Psalm 120

I PRAY FOR THE CHILDREN
of the incarcerated,
those whose parents are behind bars,
and those whose parents should be behind bars;
those whose parents think children are slaves
and those who never give a thought
to their own children.
Embrace these young throwaways
as the Great Parent You are,
the One who offers love
to all with equal grace,
the One who never succumbs to favoritism.
Help those of us charged with caring
for these little ones realize
that once we are called
to this assignment,
only death frees us from responsibility.

Psalm 121

YOU INTEND for each to walk
inside personal potential.
We do not know our God-given limits
and many are afraid to glimpse them,
knowing our natural greatness
might disturb the comfort of mediocrity.
Can we sing songs of You,
exclaiming that love is
the only way worthy
of a loving Creator?
Can we see that most barriers
separating us are as artificial
as the borders extended
from political maps
into outer space?
Against all odds, let us be
who we should be,
abandoning the masks
that celebrate constraints,
never hiding the beauty
You have awarded.

Psalm 122

UP MOST of the night
with a struggling baby,
I am grateful
for Your company.
Imitating Your perfection,
I make my calling cards
patience and love seeking purity.
Never has Your anger flared
when I failed
to do as You desire.
I will not have the audacity
to lose control.
This child needs my best.
Your spirit gives me power,
makes my hands an extension
of Your compassion.
I thank you
for Your awesome consistency.

Psalm 123

I DO AS THE CYCLIST

in mountainous terrain,

gather my strength for the coming climb.

Centuries earlier, Jesus also regrouped,

where, as always, You were waiting.

He prayed to You for strength

which You awarded for the coming struggle.

In imitation of the Nazarene and

with the cyclist's determination,

I pray that I will be prepared.

Let me ascend the heights You build.

189

Psalm 124

THROUGH YOUR GRACE
my eyesight is refreshed.
I saw her embrace loneliness.
Does she, and all others like her,
realize You are the true Comforter,
the Great Spirit
who can be counted on
when all flesh falls short?
It is tempting
to believe my size fits all,
and consider myself a savior.
Teach me where my logic holds errors,
to love with unlimited patience,
and let go of myself
to flow into Compassion's stream.
If I can discover
the me You intended,
fewer of my neighbors
will drift into isolation.

Psalm 125

THE ONLY ONE I call Lord
helps me in my struggles,
enabling me to reach out
both to those who love me
and to those who abuse me.
You bring solace
when I am hard-pressed.
All things circle
back to the Center,
reminding me that my desires
never outweigh the whole.
In unity let me live my life:
my thoughts focused on You,
my words affirmation of You,
my acts a prayer,
that others will do the same.

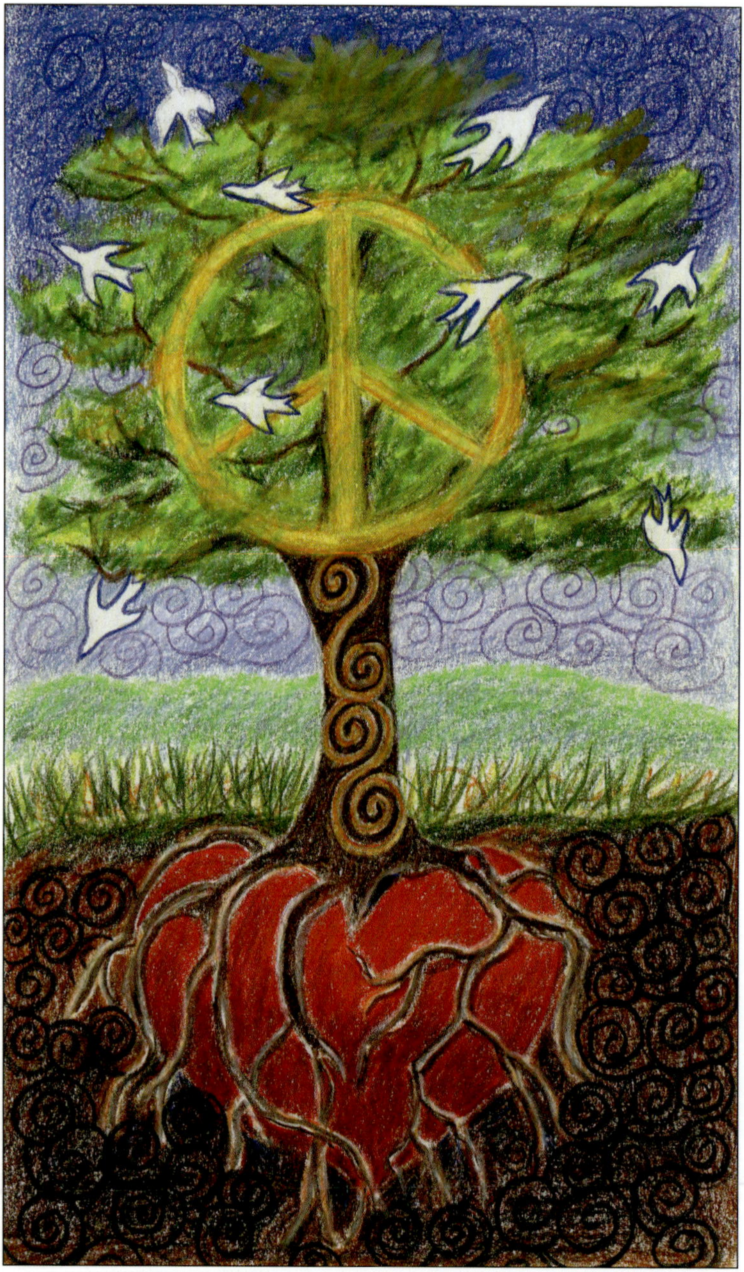

Psalm 126

THANK YOU for the gift of resilience,
the offering made to oneself.
Despite the many times we fall,
You make the season of healing
a possibility year-round.
Out of the shadow
of a thousand darknesses,
triumph has been ours.
You taught us the song of life,
and placed flowers
on an ever-blossoming tree.
We attempt to embrace,
not merely learn,
the lyrics of a song
You composed,
but we dare to refer to as "ours."
We will honor this music
so long as we breathe.

Psalm 127

IN AN EMERGENCY ROOM
waiting with yet another loved one,
I recall times past
when I feared for my own life
or that of someone near.
You arrived right on time,
singing songs of encouragement.
Again I offer gratitude
without requesting guarantees.
No doubt there were
unrecognized emergencies
when my life in this dimension
was only a breath away.
For all the occasions
when You were there,
I offer thanks
and renew my commitment
to serve as Your soldier.

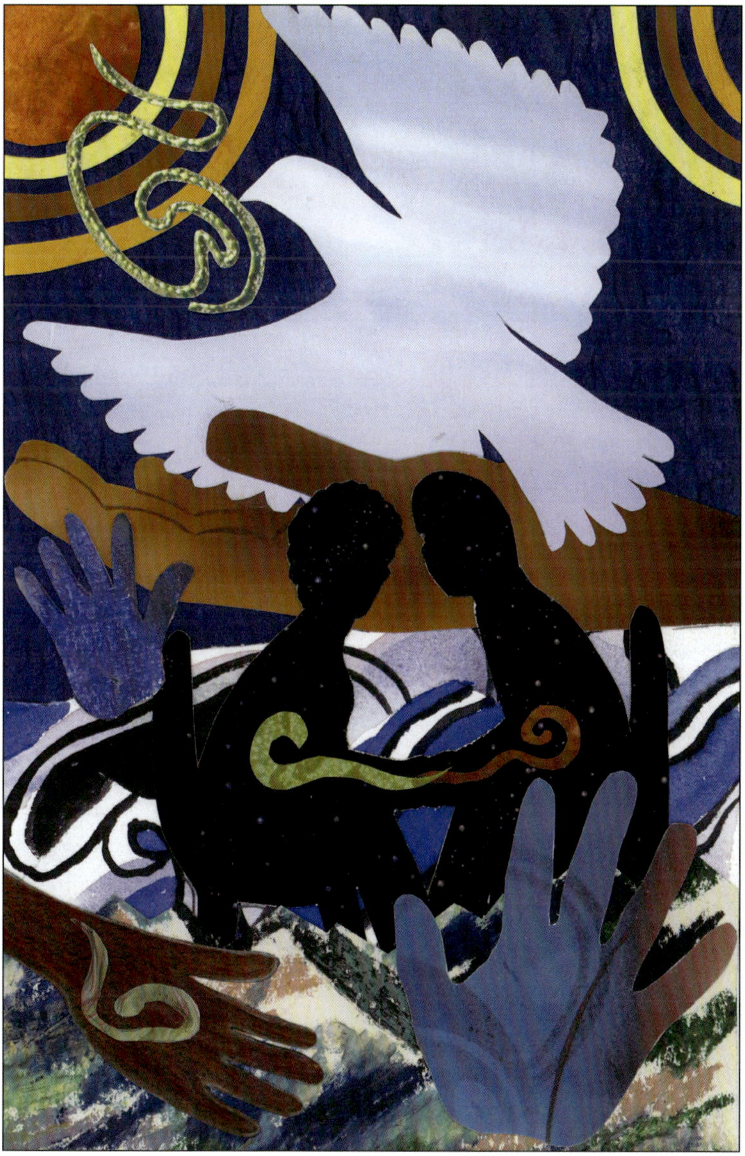

Psalm 128

ATTENDING an interfaith service
amidst a medley of believers,
I bow my head
still seeing hues of many colors.
In prayer I listen for Your voice
to help us not sell any
of our siblings
to the highest bidder.
Opening my eyes I hear speaking.
This gathering
sounds like a tower of clarity.
Each one praises Your holy essence.
We are the blessed even when persecuted.
The smallest kindness energizes Your work.
United we stand by Your grace.
The divisions that immobilized
the closed-minded have failed to conquer.
We remember that by being chosen
our only privilege is to bear
more weight in the service of healing.
Blessed are we. Blessed are You.

Psalm 129

MY ENEMIES surrounded me
wearing false smiles.
Through my naiveté
I missed the plot.
They had everything planned
except what to do if I did not die.
Through their naiveté
I am stronger than ever.
You are my Redeemer,
the One Who Enables
rebirth after the strike.
Wounded, I crossed miles of barren emptiness,
and windswept sorrow.

Your love filled every inch,
denying loneliness the slightest foothold.
With Your assistance I gathered myself
while hanging like some strange fruit
above unleashed hellhounds
licking their lips in savage anticipation.
My soul looks back and wonders about nothing.
I know through You
I found peace.

Psalm 130

LIKE THE HOSPITALIZED BABY
whose laughter is ecstatic
when Mom appears,
Your love fuels my joy.
I am excited by rebirth—
whether it's the prodigal's return, or
a newborn's emergence
from the original dimension.
The beginning is cherished
for the moment,
cherished for the certainty
that possibilities exist,
cherished because the work of ancestors
made it all possible.
Some speak of found money,
and others celebrate
the legacy windfall.
I sing of love refreshed,
realized beauty.

Psalm 131

OUR ANCESTORS TAUGHT
the fear of the Lord
is the beginning of wisdom.
Our age teaches the fear of death
is the beginning of wisdom.
There is more to You than fear.
There is worse than death.
We sing of loving You as the Strengthener.
Through oppression and disdain,
You are the One whose sorrow we fear
to bring by doing evil to our siblings
and destruction to nature.

Extended life that allows for
little more than breathing,
and hopefully contemplating,
is not always the answer.
Death has no sting to those
who find peace in Your arms.
You are the Alpha and the Omega,
the Endless One,
the Love of My Life.
All praise to You.

Psalm 132

THEY ARE POISED like gunners
in a tree house, hunting deer.
The most satisfying targets are antlered.
Into the breach You walk, declaring,
"I own this meadow.
Disarm, and find your way to peace."
Although many turn a deaf ear,
our fortitude is bolstered.
Although we are denied grazing rights
on common grounds,
harassed and pursued
in our own neighborhoods,
in You we have a merciful shield.
Hold us like a parent holds a newborn.
We do not deceive ourselves;
all are vulnerable without Your protection.

Psalm 133

OPPRESSION is not a carousel
complete with uplifting tunes.
It is a plunge into a pit
from which many will never escape.
Send us Your love-woven lifeline.
You are the One who demands justice,
as fundamental to existence.
Instead of dizzily wringing our hands,
help us advance Your cause.
We understand
that if we will not assert for ourselves,
we forfeit the right to ask You
to contend on our behalf.

Psalm 134

KEEPING THE DIVINE on hold
overlooks that the right hour is now.
Forgive us when we wait to tackle
the immovable object.
Forgive us when we pray
that some other will attend
to the obvious need.
With Your aid we can ripple
even a frozen pool.
Let us tie our cables
to the problem and pull.
Together.

Psalm 135

FORGIVE US in our strivings
when two or more
fight against Your flawless will,
neither having the courage or wisdom
to answer Your call,
both claiming You
are on our side.
Help us own ourselves with grace,
not using privilege to persecute,
ability to deconstruct,
or handicap to look past seeking assistance.
Forgive us our debts
as we try to repay our indebtedness.
Gift us when we are persecuted.
Let them know You desire our inclusion.
For Yours is all that is or ever will be,
and ours no more than a passing cloud.

Psalm 136

WHEN THE UPPER classes moved
out of declining cities,
we were angered.
Despite the nation's wealth,
the decay accelerated.
In the places
where the upper classes returned,
we were angered
for the improvements were limited.
They ask, "What do you people want?"
They close their ears to Your words,
"What I require is to do justice,
love kindness, and walk humbly."

When some are allowed

to leave and return

at their own pleasure,

and others are stuck through

Hell and high water,

the land itself is made foreign.

Empower us with opportunity.

Make possible the fulfillment of our potential.

Our true devotion is to You.

Call us by name, Holy One, and we will answer.

208

Psalm 137

THE JOURNEY has a million detours,
one ending.
I refuse to spin away
from the love song track
implanted in each child at birth.
I sing of Your composition
with as much fervor as I did on my birth day.
To You be the glory.
When others seek tunes played
with new instrumentation,
I continue to hear the swelling sounds
of Your righteous music.
On my knees, or on the mountain top,
I praise You, asking only
that You remember
a sincere attempt
to be faithful across all terrains.

Psalm 138

IN YOUTH I listened to
the ocean's voice
ignorant of the wave's intent.
Now I know Your words
reside in the waters,
those of the deep and
those on the surface.
The swelling sea
is my bosom friend,
the source of my life,
the sustainer of my future.
Hear us sing in homage
to the pure oneness
of eternal spirit.
Should we grow tempestuous,
remind us of the calmness
with which we move
when yielding to Your love.

Psalm 139

IN THIS EXCEPTIONAL MOMENT,
I praise the opportunity
to prove myself worthy
of being called human.
With two hands I hold a baby,
looking down as she looks up.
From Your righteous bosom
to my scarred arms
is an immeasurable distance.
Momentarily I am one
with You who holds me,
understanding my weaknesses
better than I ever will.
Neither of us can make it alone.
May my focus be in line
with the tenderness you continue to give.
Your steadiness models for all
regardless of our surface differences.
The psalm is Yours.
The gift is mine.

Psalm 140

MY CREATOR and my Center,
Your presence is my joy.
Today I march in a protest line,
working to eradicate war and racism.
Yesterday I met
in a meeting for worship
beside others seeking Your will.
Tomorrow I shall be in a hospital,
holding struggling babies.
Your concept of time must be radically other.
Before the beginning. After the end.

Wherever I go, you have never left,
forgiving those in the remnant,
calling back those who have strayed,
or perhaps neither sought,
nor stumbled upon the Giver of Grace.
I volunteer my hand
to both my neighbors and strangers.
We trudge through brambles
following the Guide
whose steadying authority
denies the possibility of being lost.

Acknowledgements

DWIGHT WILSON:

In appreciation for the inspiration of Abraham Joshua Heschel, Betty-Ann Workman, Clarabel Marstaller, Diane Wilson, Elias Hicks, Elizabeth Watson, Frederick Douglass, George Fox, Hazel Wilson, James Holliman, John Woolman, Joy Jones, Leslie Ziegler, Malcolm X, Martin Luther King Jr., Mia Wilson, Obelia Nettles, Pat Turner, Paul Becker, Richard Wood, Rob Dobrusin, Sojourner Truth, Stephen Sziksai, T. Canby Jones, Ted Nixon, Tom Bodine, Toni Morrison, and Vera Simmons.

The original readers of these psalms were Alice Fredericksen, Amanda Downing, Amy Hirshberg-Alderman, Becky Morehouse, Beth Ann King, Caela Wood, Connie Ryan, Diane Wilson, Donna Hutchins, Esther Lynette Williams, Grace Fisher, Hank Peirce, James Gates, Jay Cummings, Johanna McMorrow, Karen Brown, Kelsey Crowe, Mai Spann-Wilson, Mark Wilson, Michael Wilson, Palline Plum, Paulicia Bender Williams, Shannon Ryan, Shelle Russell, and Wendy LaCapra.

Each person read a set of around twenty psalms and shared with me which were personally moving to them. I am blessed to have so many supportive friends.

NANCY MARSTALLER:

In gratitude to my family, David, Syretha, and Erik Brooks; my parents Clarabel and Louis Marstaller; and my dear friends Dwight Wilson and Kitsie Hildebrandt—all have encouraged me in art and spirit.

About the Author

Dwight L. Wilson is a retired educational executive who, early in his career, served as Pastor of Durham Friends Meeting (Maine), and General Secretary of Friends General Conference. He is the father of four sons, and grandfather of two boys and one girl. He is a committed volunteer who, among other roles, currently serves on the board of Pendle Hill, as Clerk of the Earlham School of Religion Board of Advisors, Chairman of the Subcommittee on Policing for the Ann Arbor Human Rights Commission, and weekly holds babies on the cardiac ward of C.S. Mott Children's Hospital.

About the Illustrator

Nancy Marstaller is an artist and retired middle school teacher living in Harpswell, Maine. She lives with her husband David, and they feel blessed that their grown children, Syretha and Erik, live nearby.

Of her artwork, Nancy says, "I love the process of representing what I see in the outer world, my inner life, and inspirations from others. Ever since I was a teenager I have been making artwork trying to depict my spiritual journey, and sometimes what I perceive to be humankind's journey. Perhaps at least partly because I grew up as a Quaker artist, where we worship in unadorned meetinghouses without sacred art, I wanted to put into physical form some representation of spiritual experience."